What Drifted Here

Also by Barbara Siegel Carlson

Books

Once in Every Language
Take Five (with four other poets)
Fire Road

Chapbooks

Between the Hours
Between this Quivering

Translations

Open: Selected Poems and Thoughts of Srečko Kosovel (Slovene, with
Ana Jelnikar)
Look Back, Look Ahead: Selected Poems of Srečko Kosovel (Slovene, with
Ana Jelnikar)

Anthology

A Bridge of Voices: Contemporary Slovene Poetry and Perspectives (co-
edited with Richard Jackson)

What Drifted Here

Poems by Barbara Siegel Carlson

Cherry Grove Collections

For Aunt Margot,
with love & happiness for you
Barb

March 2023

Published by Cherry Grove Collections
PO Box 541106
Cincinnati, OH 45254-1106

ISBN: 9781625494245

Poetry Editor: Kevin Walzer
Business Editor: Lori Jareo

Visit us on the web at www.cherry-grove.com

Cover photo: Barbara Siegel Carlson

Author photo: Lily Stone

ACKNOWLEDGMENTS

Thanks to the following publication in which the poems below first appeared, sometimes in slightly different form.

American Journal of Poetry "Pip in the Waves"

Apokalipsa (Slovenia) "Accordion Player," "Mahler," "After a Terrorist Attack" and "Road to the Castle"

Burningword Literary Journal "A Sign"

Cutthroat "Bora" and "Locked in the Marble" ("Under the Leaves")

Mid-American Review "Sharm-el Sheikh: The Secret of Things"

The Poetry Porch "Descent," "Liminal Street," Arthur (Boo) Radley Speaks," "Still," "Pinhole" and "Intimate Stranger"

Solstice: a magazine of diverse voices "The Deepening," "Paul's Realization"

Lily Poetry Review and poems2go "Joseph Cornell Tries to Explain"

Literatura (Slovenia) "In a Silent Time," "For the Erased" and "On Questions"

the tiny journal "To My Office Manager, from Gregor" and "Melville Responds to Supersymmetry"

I am grateful to Mary Kane, Scott Withiam, Ana Jelnkiar, Miriam Drev, Miriam O'Neal and Dzvinia Orlowsky for their friendship and insights through the years; to Deborah Brown, Susan Thomas and Laura Baird, for their critical eyes in several of these poems; to Richard Jackson for his further vision; and to Larry, my family and the friends I am blessed to have.

Many thanks to Kevin Walzer and Lori Jareo of WordTech Communications for giving this manuscript a home, and for providing their technical expertise and support so generously.

For Mason, Ari, Temple and Willow

Table of Contents

Oh the infernal color of my passions.
But I remained captive to the ancient tenderness.
—Alexandra Pizarnik

I. Whose Silence

Whose silence are you?
—Thomas Merton

In a Silent Time

I came to the river's edge to sit by the gate
where water pours down in green translucence.
Its constant falling appeared still,
but the roar silenced everything—a bus
rolled over the bridge, people on the other side
ate and conversed, their mouths opening and closing,
opening and closing, tiny blue flowers
along the grassy bank nodded
to tiny blue flowers
on the other side. Between us
the deafening train of water
coursed without end—
I wanted to fill the emptiness
in those hours, join
the breathing of the man opposite me
who moved his baby carriage back and forth, back
and forth to quell perhaps a similar longing
in a place of silence so loud.

Traces

They were the first trails, these branches
making their way into the sky.
Creating their own passage,
traveling without being noticed,
transforming the air into the ways of wood.
How far they can reach in a lifetime is
anyone's guess. On clear nights
under a full moon, they make a fine
netting. A spider web whose filaments weave
in every direction. The trails grow thinner
the higher they reach. The work is never complete.
What do the dark lines seek?
How do you follow such intricate crossings?
Maybe these traces are all
the markings we have to connect.

Descent

A man is playing solitaire as we begin
our descent. Taps his thumb on each
numbered heart and spade on his phone.
To his right out the window
a steel wing. At this moment I remember
the ceiling at the airport where the security
lines form. The ceiling painted blue with clouds,
so we have something to look at as we remove
our shoes and belts, empty our pockets,
put our hands over our heads for the camera.
The man playing solitaire doesn't look out.
His reddish beard twitches. He has
a tattoo of a Chinese sign on his wrist.
Out the window the horizon's streaked green
between nothing and nothing. Below us
the world's cloaked in darkness as the plane
plunges through a cloud. The aisle is lit.
We're all buckled in—for a moment
our shoulders touch. But we're unreadable,
our lives invisible to each other
who see only the surface of things.

Mahler

Ljubljana

At Dvorni Square I meet him in a bronze statue, slender hand
over his heart. It looks like he's carrying a harp that grew from a
wound in his chest. His shoulders are bent, head leaning forward,
eyes looking down as if he hears the ripple of strings between the
hum of bicycle wheels, voices and footsteps. No one else seems to
notice it beyond the restaurant tables. Most of our lives are spent
alone and in silence, waiting to be touched. A leaf drops into the
river below between bare tarnished branches, and the river takes
it on its singular journey.

Where the Map is Cropped, the Real Place Begins

Go down stairs
past the silk clothes
of ancestors you hold in your blood,
then draw to the rivers,
to the tables laid bare,
of rosehips and fireweed
under the roughest passages
to where a woman once burrowed
inside a freshly killed moose
to stay alive
for all she couldn't hold.

Manifesto of the Crumbling Shed

Before me is continually an empty space
—Kierkegaard

The windows are cloudy, frames charred, roof drafty with leaves. Winter buds hard as bullets sway over. Who else hears the twigs quiver? Mahler walked through storms as a boy feeling their crashes, rhythms and laments as if they were the notes of his own estranged soul under branches that crack as they reach toward the sky.

Maybe I'm just hungry for mystical connections. How to be boundless inside these webs, rusty tools, pots with the dirt still clinging, while I sink into the slope between house and swamp, wondering where does the wild begin, how do my walls dry in the wind, how can the feather that landed on my threshold be understood.

Provisional

Thousands of webs are cast
across the weeds at the pond's edge
At dawn they're all
covered in dew each milky strand
Each web from a different spider
each one a solitary creation that shudders
and sways in the breeze
This must be the great secret
—how each creates a way
to capture what it needs
and lets the rest blow through
A spider lurks unseen in every corner
waiting as the clouds flow by

Letter to Kierkegaard From Dickinson

I have more birds in my life than people
Today I'm looking for them—Tapestries of Sound—
But the Birdbath's full of Leaves
You say *become Joy*
Like the Bird that sings of Nothing
And the Lily that drinks God in Light—My Words
My only Wings
Without them who
Would note this Breath? What Flower
Would rise without Earth? For the Emptiness
Is Fathomless—
I'm searching for Joy in the Blankness of the Sky
Between my Arms—though I can't
Penetrate a Soul
Or hold a Bird in Flight

At the Aquarium

I see it feelingly.
—Gloucester, *King Lear*

I'm buried in the world like you, octopus with your 3 hearts. You that can fit through a crack as thin as the eye and tell one human face from another. You know the sea feeds every urchin and all the others swimming are within your grasp. You move through currents, feel the vibration of the train along the coast, the rambling of the homeless in their fitful sleep and quivers of the wounded and the dying. How your arms uncoil and slip through the miles as the voices of those all around us. You don't wonder where the screaming and the moaning go. Nor do you drown in the towering waves. Who knows what the eyes in your hearts see, the mouths in your arms taste—Whose soul reaches past the tip of each tendril for its reckoning, as much as it beckons, though no one responds?

What Drifted Here

Only a fragment of any story can be gathered. No one saw the young boy slip back into the water and drown. It's impossible to hear what licks the water today. A fly dropped like stone dust from a cliff. Each wing a language of journey. A man crept into a backyard where friends were having dinner and held a gun to one of the women's heads. Another woman offered the man a glass of wine. He took a sip, then said he was sorry and asked for a hug. I don't know who I am or what I can whisper to save us. Pope Francis was silent at Auschwitz. Near him stood an old woman who as a child played the violin at the death camp. Each note of the heart goes out. Every morning I sweep up these crumbs. Every morning the dark turns light to see something small.

Melville Responds to Supersymmetry

I do believe we shimmer
when the particles collide—
How the earth must seek
its distant spark *while the brain*
eats out the heart. (My thoughts
like Ahab's *truth*
hath no confines.) We wander the waves
as cannibals and saints, our tattoos
and scars mapped from a cosmos
we'll never solve, but such mysteries
take us to the core of what
we are: particles with shadow ones
unknown to us, sister souls
spinning at a frequency
we can't detect, Bartleby's gloom
and Pip's vision interred in the waves
we unwittingly cast that will drown us
into a different form. Our photons
stream through solar maelstroms.
Even the whale's inviolate boom and wake
are hologram in space, as all of us
orphans on a universal raft
of dark matter, some vast
and imperceptible solitude
that has no tongue.

The Deepening

It's as if each morning were a pool into which
I have been lowered. Or I dove in and now sit
on my blue sofa at the bottom of the sky, swathed
in a milky substance amid the trilling of crickets.

A few minutes ago my husband clinked his spoon
to his cereal bowl, then stepped to the sink
to wash them. Soon the side door opened
and closed, and he was gone.

In my pool the dream of sleeping in a tiny room
whose walls started softening with wastewater
felt all too real. The truth is both milky and dirty.
The truth is he didn't wash his bowl or spoon.

In a Side Room

Venice

A clock-mirror hangs on the wall
in a side room smelling of old stone
in the Frari Basilica. Face stained, surrounded
by numbers and signs of the zodiac.
The clock has no hands, the mirror a window
of faraway light. A child on its right
tries to embrace it. Another to push it away.
People stream in and out—young and passionate,
old and alone, those haunted who sleep without hours
and dream in the path of the planets
where all of our lives are entwined.

Puppet

My friend is fascinated by puppets for the way they move from bits of material. She makes them dance and fly on their strings and sticks as she runs making great sweeping motions across the night sky in a field where a terrible battle took place under the same little dipper trembling so far away.

Bora

Trieste

All night the bora wind creaked through the building and combed through the windows. What or whom was it looking for? It littered the streets to the bus station with black leaves. Only a police car crawled through the Piazza Unita past the square all lit in blue to show where the sea water once flooded. Above, a gust sent a tremor across the blue lights to the Timavo River that begins in the Karst and disappears underground until it gushes out a few miles from here on the coast at Duino. Sometimes a door bangs open and no one is there but a terrible longing.

To the One in Child's Pose at the Train Station

You're not
the statue with a gnawed-off nose,
or the breath of the hair-lipped girl
who keeps waking me
in the prayer-house with no door,
but a chandelier of human bones chiming in the middle.

If you're the gull with a gaping beak,
I'm the boy who drew himself in colored pencil,
then tore through the paper,
making holes for the eyes.

Outside the station
there's a bare tree shaking,
I can't tell
where the bird cries are coming from.

Under the Leaves

Leaves stir around
the old well that's been
covered for winter. Underground
the water flows through all
that is lost: potsherds
and bone flecks, hair
and sweat, teeth and blood.
What about voices and dreams?
Where do our memories go?
The leaves are thirsty.

II. The Lost Guiding You

The things that you lost
by the way were guiding you
—W.S. Merwin

Seeing Things

Long braids covered her face
and no one spoke or looked at her
in the crowded subway car
as she carried on saying things—
almost singsong
as though putting a child to bed—
only the voices
kept rising from forces
no one could fathom.

Just outside the station a red petal
marked with footprints
lay on the pavement,
blown from some flower
that opened in the sun
so close, so far away
whose light is all we see.

Waking in Trieste

The window is wide open at this early hour facing an abandoned lot between two buildings across the narrow street. The overgrown brush undulates and branches of a plane tree sway in gusts. From far off come the mews of a gull. It feels almost like a sanctuary. I think of the nuns in medieval times cloistered in their cells for love of God. Each with a space no one could fathom in the stillness between walls. And prisoners in solitary confinement, what must come through the constant wind as it sighs to the forgotten and bends the tall grasses.

Post-truth

I pause by a hill
rustling with vines
between a ripped trunk
and broken limbs
a twig wags
what's buried
out of view
every voice
trembles the air
every word
is dropped
like a leaf to the ground
the phantoms all gather
their torn-out song

Dawn Remains

The pile of roots and stumps pulled from the pond seems to
breathe. Some of the driftwood is bleached, other branches
charred, twisted into some strange dance from their marrow of
heat, reminiscent of limbs in a pile outside a Civil War hospital.
People believe in their own immortality, sway over unmarked
graves. Under clouds, in the fumes of churned earth, breath
becomes mist that encloses each violet bud.

> Our bodies are lost
> in a field of hungry birds
> and the songs they sing.

Arthur (Boo) Radley Speaks

It was myself I wanted to cut loose
from the rope like the one
round the neck of a man
swaying from a branch.
I couldn't breathe when I saw
what runs from a body.
Maybe I carved the soap dolls
to wash the blood from my own hands.
But everyone wears a hard
shell of a costume,
and sometimes it saves you.
How do you wash the blindness
from a man's eyes? I couldn't speak
because truth has no color or voice,
but it melts like soap and grows clear
in the darkness between the walls,
until the walls disappear.

To a Hill of Dirty Snow in the Parking Lot

The inflatable man lies face down in the snow and the Colonel is still smiling on the red KFC sign that tilts to one side. I'm listening to the news about the death of the cardinal who preached unity and reconciliation while protecting his pedophilic priests. Little mounds of dirty snow, your cousins lie under the shrubbery in front of the low brick Washington Arms. Who else says one thing to hide something else? I smile at the stuffed antlers poking out of the van windows in front of me and the squirrel running across the powerline above this street of stalled traffic. And there you are, stained with every passerby's exhaust as you melt to the ground.

Accordion Player

Ljubljana

He sits on a stool covered with sheepskin, his eyes
behind dark glasses, his accordion expanding,
contracting. Dressed in lederhosen,
he plays a polka as everyone strolls
past: the stringy-haired woman
whispering to herself, a man in a striped fedora
carrying a loaf of bread, a baby poking
its big dark eyes out of a hat, while the young
mother in tight jeans wheels past a heavy-set girl
in a black apron. Now a man with one arm
walks by a cart of balloons. The tune
grows merrier, the bobbing head
of a white pigeon seems part of the music.
As well, the gray pigeon whose breast is purplish, as if
the heart had bled through and stained all the feathers.

Sharm-el Sheikh: The Secret of Things

It was before the October War.
I was riding a bus to the sea.
I met a soldier there and we ate oranges in the sand.
The next day he gave me a dog carved out of olive wood.
I wrapped the dog in my towel.

Years later when I had my own home,
I placed it on a high shelf where it has sat
bathed in every hue of darkness and light,
the room full of voices and silence.

The soldier's eyes looked like pieces of sea glass.
I remember his fingers that were the first ones
inside me. The water a legendary turquoise.
Somewhere his plane went down.

Today there's still war, another plane crash
and Sharm-el-Sheikh turning into a ghost town.
For the first time I wash the dog,
and rubbing it dry, remember how
our impressions were lifted away by a single wave.

Dark Crumbs

Ljubljana

Lights from the building windows flickered
in the furrows of water below.
As the man played his violin on the bridge
shadows spread across his gaunt face,
his longing cast into the night.
In the morning in a dug-up street
not far from where the man had stood,
a woman brushed at the dirt
beside several other orange-suited workers
digging in other parts of the street.
Kneeling over a skeleton,
she brushed away the dark crumbs
that hide so many hungers.

What Cannot Be Touched

A Hesychast tries to contain within his body something incorporeal.
—St Gregory

St. Petersburg

After the tsar's children were killed, their bodies were dumped in
an abandoned mine but later removed, burned and buried in
wetlands near the road in secret. It's not so easy to make a body
disappear. Even in the most brutal of deaths, something remains
that cannot be touched. In life you must be totally still for a long
time, the Hesychast believes, to see what is eternal. In a glass case
on a page from a diary kept during the Siege, a girl has written,
"I dream about porridge." The mottled brown sheet is faintly
lined. Each page is colored with suffering and dreams. Each leaf
of the heart holds a branch of its hunger. In the cathedrals
before Easter people wait in line for the priest to bless their
frosted cakes, shaking a brush of holy water at them. Their
passions a mystery. Heavy with candles and incense, the air
smells of raw mountain streams.

Road to the Castle

Ljubljana

Moss eats into the wall along the narrow cobbled road
leading to the castle. Dead vines hang over the side,
blushed and swaying. Dangling from one of the tendrils,

clusters of brown seeds cling to the silvery spirals and ghostly
skeleton of a flower. Torn leaves the color of black tea
are stuck in a web. Pigeons murmur and a leaf scrapes along.

A few homes hug the road. Decrepit windows with old bars,
dried flowers in boxes, moss hanging over gutters.
An old woman in black high-topped shoes and a fur coat

walks up the road, pauses by a gnarled tree, her white hair
a shock of brightness against the dark trunk, her mouth open
as she looks up. She continues uphill, red pocketbook

dangling from her hand. She crosses a bridge over steep
terrain, climbs the iron stairs slowly. At the top of the hill
near the castle, the old woman meets a younger one, and they hug

near a wall with a locked door. There's a crack
between the door and wall—it's the same on both sides—
a sepia tangle of branches and vines amid the cries of crows.

For the Erased

Ljubljana

In the Rog Factory yard there's a plaster
statue of a man with a word
in Russian scrawled on his back.
The rusty wire hair
made of old box springs
has a green gun nestled inside.
His cheek holds a cobweb
with a tiny spider.
Sitting in a vinyl chair in the middle
of a weed patch
surrounded by dilapidated buildings
whose windows are black,
this hollow figure
a flower in the dark.

Along the Tracks

Blue tarp over a dirt pile,
and then a flaming brush pile

clears into brown patches of gardens.
A man in purple pants holds a bundle of

forsythia branches that glow
for a moment. I'm sitting backwards

on the train, my arms thirsty,
my legs vibrating with rushing sounds,

while a stranger crosses the field
with a shadow that makes no sound

but the dark flame never leaves.

Still

after Anne Frank

So still as to feel a wall breathe
like paper before flames. Plates
on the other side still cold, still perfect
as placed in the cupboard. Still
later at the camp, as one of your own
tore bread from your hands. Are you still
near the border, starved as the enemy?
Still a stream of light that the dust floats on,
waiting for the kind people, and beautiful baskets
of strawberries, and your dear Pim—still
under all the layers of clothes
worn into hiding—and still wearing those pajamas
crawling with bugs. Whose voices
were shaken when something glittered
again and again to still some smaller
more infinite grain?

Liminal Street

St Petersburg

Crow on a wire above the snowy street,
where do you sleep? I can't see
any green. Why that guttural cry
as you sweep down
to drink from a puddle.
You don't wonder who lives
or lived in one of these
pastel buildings that face each other
in the shadow of the cathedral,
who climbs that staircase,
who warmed themselves on their books,
who sits at the window
with nothing in her pockets
and no place to call home.

After a Terrorist Attack
November 2015

The city square is buried in leaves. I pick up a yellow one, almost weightless but limp in my hand like the yellow star my friend showed me once—its thin cloth held in her palm—the star her father was forced to wear over his heart. I touched the tiny stitch holes around each point. What is it the holes can't say? The leaves whisper around my feet. More are shaken down and people trample them: the man smoking a cigarette, the mother pushing a stroller, the guy staring at his cell phone.

Undocumented

A doll's shoe washed up on the beach, a high-top with no laces over an empty tongue. Who played with it, lost it, forgot about it, maybe threw it into the waves like a child in a storm between the waves that rose and fell? The waves like a train take you to your parents, to where they are hidden. Where are their voices? The one you lost still dreams.

> For a while it bobbed,
> little boat on the ocean,
> carrying no one.

Lament for the Lost Ones

Once a whale with a swollen tongue
washed up on the beach

a tongue that seeped into the sand
opening each night

to receive the floodwaters
and those bodies

riddled and rippling with holes
you can't tell one

body from another
one hole from another

heart from the heartless

Dear Dead Man

After everyone leaves I see you in the mirror
as the wind without any tree. Your religion must be snow,
your statement concrete, your city the burnt-out sockets
of parking lights. Your constellation of emptiness hurtling
light years away will never touch down, though it passes
right through me. Thanks for the dead lady's coat.
In the pockets a few scabs and old fingernails. You left me
all these empty frames, some negatives and invisible ink,
and words that bleed. For you it is never too complicated—
your pin won't expire nor your password be condemned;
like afternoon shadows, we can't ever stop kissing—
one bruise now yellow-green as a Granny Smith apple.
Soon I too will vanish into a chime. Is it you, my love,
speaking through the white pigeon's black freckles?
I didn't ask to speak through the lost souls that stream
out my eyes. But both of us know *the darker you become,*
the more touching. Because there is only one sky, one
crackling voice, one pantomime whose mouth is filled with air,
so the inflatable man called "The Scream" still screams
on my neighbor's front lawn, while silence covers the loudest
passion and bells that reverberate to the insatiable go on.

III. Threshold

A threshold opens up behind your footprints

—Adonis

Poet Sprouting Roots

Inspired by Ali Ahmad Sa'id (Adonis) b.1930

i.

We come from the woods and sky
burning with stars from unreachable voids
where darkness enters our blood,
but the heart, that's a collection
of shadow-less laments under wet leaves
and the yearnings of a world
whose language covers us
as some dark river rushing
with all that can never be said,
which is most of what we are.
And rocks with their monkey faces
and the rooster crowing by the river
to the holes in the reddening leaves
whose breath is our teacher.

ii.

Breath carries our mystery,
merging with the wind and dark
that penetrate each dream
and the *voice of the wound*
grows as a country mired in lies.

I listen to cars sweep down the street
and late summer wings in the night.
Both sound from a source
that is just a momentary rising
of notes delirious as the calls of coyotes.

iii.

Your words enter
and leave me speechless,
seeping like rain
into *these caves under the skin,*
these dams, these ruins.

You transmute words to music
whose meaning's unknown
and unforgettable. You hold what is
already in my blood
flowing to no sound.

iv.

O language of the rubble,
O halo of dead angels,
where the lost now live,
in those luminous places
the torturers and greedy can't see.

And when you say *loss is a radiance*
the face of the wind is nothing
but the sheen of a wave
as the love we hold,
we hold to our death.

v.

I look *toward the land of bewildered clarity*
for your space in the movement of dust
as light deepens in darkness,

and when I open my eyes to where
all the days and nights breathe
every path is dissolved.

IV. You Breathed on My Hands

You breathed
on my hands so I could play
—Frank Stanford

Silent Rhapsody

How can I express what it meant
to pull up the blinds
on the door leading out to the small
wooden porch to find
a tiny guitar made of spider silk
wrapped around a piece of string?

The guitar has two arms of silk—
one clings to a chime
under a clay angel, the other
reaches out to nothing
and waves wildly.

Sylvia and the Stranger

Sylvia cannot speak; she cannot tell the heron's secret and give its life away.
—*The White Heron,* Sarah Orne Jewett

Sometimes the sun sets a white flame on the water
and you can still feel the heat
long after dark and the birds go silent.

My lightest step on a forest twig
would make the white bird sail away.

Still I held you
as the forest holds its children.

When I lifted your bag, it was heavy
with birds.

All night I lay awake with my secret
hidden in a dead tree,
my arms empty.

Next morning I climbed
through branches of the tallest pine
and spotted the white bird as it opened its wings,
crying for what I could not.

Letters from Gregor

i.   To My Sister Grete

When you pushed a chair to the window
I thought you understood
I was still there under the sheet.
The desk was all I had left.
The lady in furs framed on the wall
was all I had known
of real love, so I clung to the glass
as though there was something underneath,
even as the hospital turned to fog out the window,
even as the mound under blankets in a doorway
locked in his own unraveling.
When my mouth stopped working
I called and called
for someone to lift the blanket.

ii.   To My Father, from Gregor

The walls I couldn't knock down,
though Mother's voice made a tiny crack,
even as the membranes between us
thickened with dirt and smelled of the past.
Words locked in my throat,
my shell sealed with resin.
(How could you know it was
my breath in that cold room?)
When you bolted the door
to hide me further away, only then
in the stillness and distance
as Grete played her violin
my shell shuddered, then cracked
from the music
that watered and warmed

what was broken in me.

iii.   To My Office Manager

You couldn't see what I was
cut from, the stranded things
that filled my day: a flicker
of the tram along the wall,
clouds moving toward oblivion.
How long had I sat at my desk,
figuring without realizing I had been
taken by those who had long buried
their unknown parts. Maybe that's why
Kafka made me an insect
without a name, a shadowy creature
hidden in a room without a lamp
or map. And what you created in your blindness
was someone I couldn't find in myself.
Maybe it's best to have a shell
inscribed with memories and hungers,
even if they have nowhere to go—
For after everyone leaves,
and your family shuts the door,
an inexplicable wind
takes you into the radiance
of all that is buried.

Paul's Realization

As he fell, the folly of his haste occurred to him with merciless clearness, the
vastness of what he had left undone.
—*Paul's Case,* Willa Cather

The images were all I ever I wanted—
to be lost inside the blueness
of a painting whose setting reflects
everything we cannot say. Or the symphony
as it floats up through the elevator shaft,
the wild strains of music releasing me
to other worlds. I could've kept going,
past my father's parlor and the neighbors'
judging eyes—to breathe in the quiet of the violets
lost in snow, to be touched by the secret light
of the dusky leaves just before they darken.
I could've composed the rush that comes
when the curtain opens and a story unfolds.
I could've loved the moments
when I leaned against the window,
watching the white grains vanish into glass,
but I believed the pleading eyes
of the toothless old woman holding her red flower
out to me—I couldn't see the brutal streets
that led her there, or the dream that has no roots,
and I wondered what it is that hungers
for our lost and famished souls
to blossom in another way.

On Utopia Parkway

After Joseph Cornell

On my morning walk a marble rolled up to my feet.
The wings shimmered inside.
Now blank paper gazes in from the window.

A gondolier glides through the door,
and in the corner a violin opens its mouth
to a cockatoo on its paper perch.

My teachers are dancers. One of them
taught me how to decorate a cake with a wand.

When the sweetness crumbles into sadness,
there's the music of Schubert—his early death
lighting the top of the stairs, stars coming in.

In the living room filled with unwritten songs,
my brother sketches each small creature,
humming in his wheelchair.

Nights he fingers the strings
until the notes left by the starlings find me.

In Rooms of Solitude

The lapis lazuli table made of fragments
looks like an inscrutable map of consciousness
over many lifetimes. In another room
Rembrandt's old face has disappeared
into the cracked paint. We stroll through the Gallery
of Heroes, pass over names in the frames
left blank. It would take nine years
to see everything in these hundred rooms.
It was called *Hermitage* because
you could be a hermit inside, wander alone
across fourteen different woods, a kaleidoscope
of rays through the window, all the white shadows,
mirages and slivers of selves
that coalesce from the stars.

Pip in the Waves

He saw God's foot upon the treadle of the loom and spoke it.
—Moby Dick, Herman Melville

Left in the endlessness beyond
the tangled lines
and the boats just specks, I drowned
and found the water as sky at sunrise,
and in the clouds hanging purple, the world
of waves falling and rising
over me, my mother's hand
I wouldn't let go—was it her
whispering from the brightest sand?

She told me about a fish
that spit out a man. Thirsty
in its blind skin, it hunts me down,
I can't lift my arms—my mouth
falls apart— *Ungraspable phantom,*
are you what pulls me
to the bottom or lifts me up?
What will sink this floating ship
shadows it, guiding it
into the emptiness of the glittering drops.

A Sign

My father came to sit on the blue wicker stool in the upstairs
bathroom of my childhood home. Talking in his familiar voice as
if he'd been alive the whole time in another place. I finally asked
him the question I most wanted to ask before he died. He said I
feel it whenever you pray for me, he who never understood what
it meant to pray. He said it feels like deep silk. I didn't
understand, but I did. I asked him to give me a sign that he
heard me when he returned to wherever he had to go. He
repeated it feels like deep silk, my home.

To the Road

You carry us on your back
but can't feel our legs
turning to water, our bodies to earth,
as you lie under the lost
colors of a blackbird
pecking at a puddle. In one place
you sparkle with shards.
Your cracks tell part
of a story. Maybe
you're trying to reach
the leaves pressed to one side
or the other, or follow the ones
that lift in a gust to be carried.

Follain

As I was reading your book with the poem about red ice and the girl who will die young being called into supper and *one whose body will always be lonely,* a tiny red insect appeared on the page called "The Children." It walked across the words and white space to the corner and did not leave.

Near Raskolnikov's House

...all the dream characters dream, too
—Schopenhauer

Dostoyevsky saw Petersburg as a puppet theater haunted by
ghosts and strange dreamers. Later it was an invisible city of
sexless people starving in their beds, listening to the ticking of a
metronome, digging up snow in the street. Today it's a white-
haired woman dangling her pocketbook, a man in a cap who
drinks from a bottle he puts back in his coat. Others in fur and
thick scarves who step through the slush, flicking their ashes. One
in the costume of a cow. You don't know who's being hunted,
who has the tremors, who pulls their dead on imaginary sleds. Or
what draws you to the channel whose dark water flows with
everything that seeps in.

Love Song

In one corner, an antique chair cries to the geese at dawn,
urgency involving promises. The resonant tang
of coyotes' screams. In another corner, a man's pet spider
weaves. Light years away a planet glistens to the ground. Everything
happens with clarity in-between. Whales hear other whales
thousands of miles away calling through the vastness
of interminable days under cover of ice and shadows
of unseen ships. No two songs ever the same. We don't meet
on a map. When you fold and unfold it too many times it grows wings.

On Questions

Some men ask questions to test you and when you don't know
the answer you don't know whether they love you more or less.
They love to ask another question. Strange how the game can
continue for decades, how it can be passed down like a gift for
singing, telling a joke or finding lost things. I was walking in the
old quarter of Ljubljana and found a paintbrush on a ledge by
the river. I wanted to ask it what it had painted to leave such
bright yellow speckles on its handle. Later, passing by a remnant
of a wall left over from Roman times, I glimpsed an old woman
selling bouquets of lavender, smiling to herself.

Intimate Stranger

You don't look at me directly
        only a glance across the table
Your black coffee eyes hold time
        lost before and after us
half filled with an intoxicating drink
        Your voice hushed as mine—
Is it rain, relief or grief
        that flows through every street?
And still I walk with you
        past dark shoe shops, cafés
and clinking glasses
        to an empty table
Here we sip some wine
        A few drops stain the night stones

Pinhole

I found a stain on my pillow,
a purple freckle.
Every night I rubbed it awake.
Inside the stain was another
and another
darker, deeper.
It wasn't a stain but a pore
of imperceptible dimension
that I couldn't pry open.
I can't tell you why
that thread-less place
mattered so much.

Lodge

Gakona, Alaska

Caribou, mouth sewn shut, nostrils flared.
On the adjacent wall the head of a wolf,
mouth open, tongue a thick red petal
in the shape of a heart, rippled, resting
between fangs. The black nose stippled,
yellow eyes reflect what is still in the room.
The wind that will never stop calling.

Joseph Cornell Dreams by the Stove

He wore bandages of moonlight
and stood at the edge of an abyss.
Behind the stove glass a dancer
without a stage wandered
in search of a fountain, heart running
to the sea. He followed the glowing
embers of a ship sighing between
hushed whales to the bones of those
lost at sea, now filled with voices
he had not heard before
or had forgotten, who were calling
as they have always called, only now
he could hear them
from the stillness under the waves.

The Bubble

Born from the wave of a wand
in a woman's hand. Its body sheer colors
that shift and wobble over the sticky hands
of the children who want to catch it. But it won't obey.
It won't become a pet, a necklace, a friend. It roils
its luminous belly from side to side reflecting the visions
in people's eyes as it floats on the breeze without making
a sound. It sails between signs, rises over the fence, glides
past the upper windows and slips through the wires.
It surpasses the church spire, the birds, the clouds.
When and where its diaphanous skin will vanish
are anyone's guess. Our eyes held captive by such
a graceful ascent to become nothing.

Your Martian Sea

I can't drink the water
taste the otherworldly salt
enter a pocket
of your frozen sea

in the years of light
swirling of no speech
in your voice

How can I know
who breathes
out of my body's
infinite hollow

to reach yours

Silla

There is neither gain nor loss in the mountain and the river.
–Muso Soseki

This is what I must remember.
The mountain is covered in mist.
Some of the trees look like ghosts
and the river below is full of risings
that cannot be seen in the light of day.
It is with its essence that is
no more than a sip of water.

Joseph Cornell Tries to Explain

I loved each bead with its hole.
Every Cracker Jack toy has a story
that whispered to me as a bookmark
in a dream, a place I could lie down inside
where the blinds have cracks
and moonlight whitens the floor boards.
Because each symphony starts
with the movement of an ant
taking its grain of sugar back
to its home in the hole between voices.
Under the quince tree's falling leaves
I lost myself, and my breath
couldn't hold onto or let go of the bodies
of the stars that tore through it.

Notes

For the Erased
The Rog Factory was a bicycle factory in Ljubljana used as a cultural, artistic and social center bringing artists and activists together from 2006 to 2021 when it was forcefully shut down by city authorities.

Dear Deadman
Italicized lines are by Anna Akhmatova

Poet sprouting roots
The title is from Adonis's elegy to the early Sufi figure Al-Hallâj who was executed in 222 A.D. for blasphemy for the mystical statement "I am the Truth."

All italicized passages are taken from *Mihyar of Damascus: His Songs* by Adonis, Translated by Adnan Haydar and Michael Beard, BOA, 2008.

Silla
Silla was an ancient and remote kingdom uniting Korea.

About the Author

Barbara Siegel Carlson is the author of two books of poems *Once in Every Language* and *Fire Road,* and the chapbook *Between the Hours*; co-translator (with Ana Jelnikar) *of Look Back, Look Ahead: Selected Poems of Srečko Kosovel*; and co-editor (with Richard Jackson) of *A Bridge of Voices: Contemporary Slovene Poetry and Perspectives.* She has published poems, translations and articles in the US and abroad. Carlson is Poetry in Translation Editor of *Solstice: a literary magazine of diverse voices*, teaches in Boston and lives in Carver, Massachusetts.